The REAL Scientist Investigates...

SPACE

Peter Riley

SEA-TO-SEA

Mankato Collingwood London

Contents

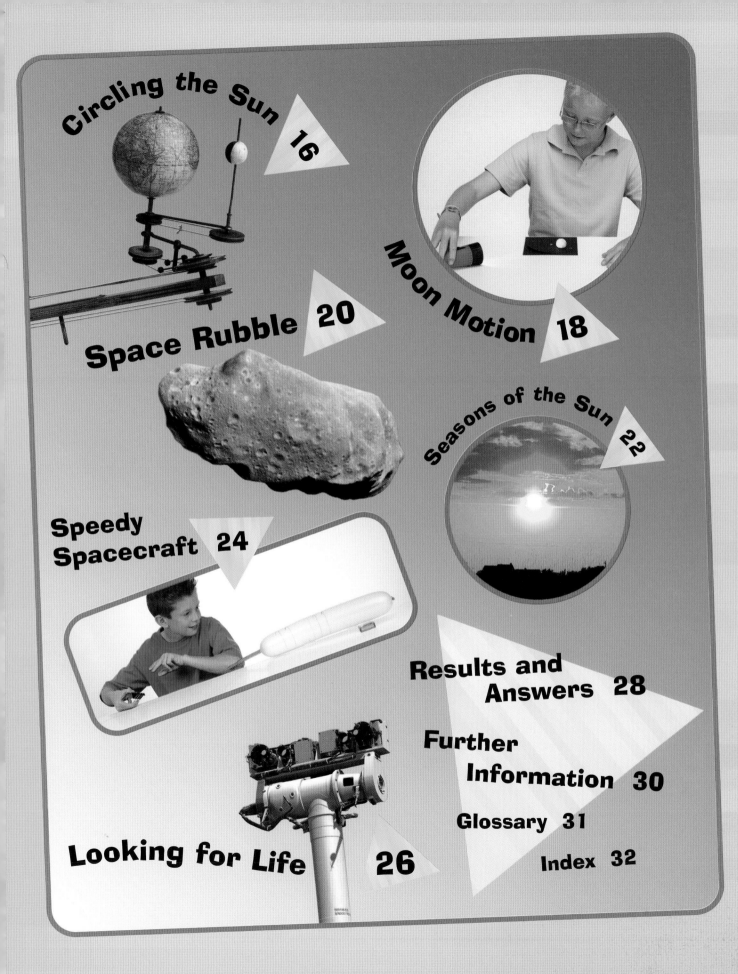

Super Solar System

When you look up at the sky at night, you are actually looking out into space. On a clear night you can see the stars, the Moon, and even other planets. They are all part of what real scientists call the solar system. Our planet Earth is also in the solar system. Along with the other planets, it is spinning around a star we call the Sun.

About 14 billion years ago the solar system didn't exist—not even space itself. Most scientists believe a speck of light smaller than a pinhead appeared and suddenly exploded to a colossal size. Scientists call this the Big Bang.

With the Big Bang, stuff called matter came into existence and the universe formed. Bits of stuff became stars and planets, and energy began spinning them around and moving them through space. Today stuff and energy are still doing the same thing.

These astronauts are building the International Space Station, which orbits the Earth.

How to Be a Real Scientist

Real scientists look into space and try to understand it by thinking about it and performing experiments. You can be a real scientist too! Just look at each topic, read the "Get going" section, and then start experimenting.

Set up a Science Box

Find a large box, then look through the pages in this book to find out all the things you will need in order to get going on each activity. Gather them up and put them in your science box.

Use These Science Skills

▶ **Observe**
Look carefully at whatever you are investigating.

▶ **Predict**
Guess what will happen before you experiment.

▶ **A fair test**
If you are comparing how something in space behaves, make sure you keep everything the same in your tests except for one thing, such as the position of your model star or planet.

▶ **Science notebook**
You will need a science notebook in which to put information about your investigations.

▶ **Record**
Write down what happened and perhaps make a drawing in your science notebook. You could take photographs too or make a video using a camcorder or cellphone.

▶ **Make a conclusion**
Compare what actually happened with your prediction and see if you were right. It does not matter if you were wrong because it helps you rethink your ideas.

▶ **Experiments and answers**
Follow the steps in the experiments carefully. Use your science skills. There may be extra experiments and a question for you to try. Check all your observations, ideas and answers on pages 28–29.

▶ **What went wrong?**
Science experiments are famous for going wrong—sometimes. If your experiment does not seem to work, check the "What's wrong?" section to help you make it right.

Gassy Galaxies

At first, our universe was nothing but gas and dust. Giant clouds called galaxies swirled around, with smaller balls of gas and dust inside. The balls became very hot and began to burn and glow—they had turned into stars. There are millions of stars in a galaxy, and billions of galaxies in space.

▼ The Andromeda galaxy is the closest one to the Milky Way. We can see it on a clear night as a faint smudge in the sky.

Some galaxies swirl in a spiral pattern. Others look egg-shaped, or elliptical. The remaining galaxies form lumpy, or irregular, shapes. The galaxy we live in is a spiral one called the Milky Way.

Get Going

Since the Big Bang, many new galaxies have formed. Scientists have discovered that they are slowly spreading out because the universe is still expanding. You can see how galaxies move in the universe by blowing up a balloon.

Blow Up Universe

1 Inflate the balloon to about 1¼ in. (3 cm) across. Bend the end down and clip it to keep the air in.

Science Box

2 balloons, binder clip, gold or silver pen, measuring tape, glitter paste, shaving foam, tray, poster paint, paper.

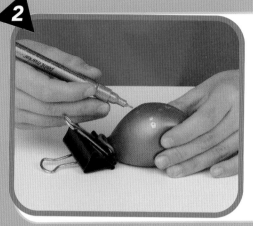

2 Use the metallic pen to draw three dots on the balloon in a triangle shape. These are your galaxies. Make sure the triangle has sides of different lengths. Label the dots A, B, and C.

▶ **Observe**
What happens to the distances between the galaxies as you blow up the first balloon?

▶ **Record**
Make a table recording the distances between the galaxies A–B, B–C, and A–C at each stage of inflation. Use a camcorder or cellphone to film your expanding universe.

3 Measure the distances between the dots. Then inflate the balloon to about 3 in. and measure again. Inflate to 4 in. (10 cm), and 5½ in. (14 cm), and measure the distances each time.

▶ **Predict**
Scientists once thought the universe would stop expanding and start contracting. What would happen then? Let the air out of the balloons to find out.

▶ **Extra experiment**
Create the effect of a spiral galaxy by spreading some shaving foam on a tray then swirling in some paint. Lay a piece of paper on top of the swirl to make a print.

4 Inflate the second balloon then let the air out. Draw sparkly galaxies all over it—remember all the different shapes. Blow up the balloon again to see your expanding universe!

Shapes in the Stars

All of the stars in our sky are part of the Milky Way. If you look carefully, you can pick out patterns among them. Real scientists call these constellations. Early people named the constellations they saw after gods, heroes, and animals. Today we have names for 88 constellations, and these are used to make maps of the sky.

▲ The four large stars here make up the Southern Cross. Light from most stars in the Milky Way takes hundreds of years to reach us.

▲ Scientists use radio telescopes, like this one, to study space.

The stars in a constellation are not as close together as they seem. Some are hundreds of light years apart. A light year is the distance traveled by a ray of light in a year—that's 5,865,696,000,000 miles in one year (9.439 million, million km)!

Get Going

Can you see patterns and pictures in the stars? Take a look one night. Draw the shapes that you see. Now try making your own constellation in a darkened room.

Cool Constellations

1 Place the table at the end of the room and put the boxes on it. Set up the flashlights, one on each box and one on the table top.

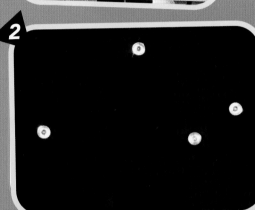

2 Switch on the flashlights, darken the room, and look at your "constellation" from the other side of the room.

▶ **Observe**
Do the stars in step 3 appear to be at different distances from you or the same distance? Do bright and dim stars appear to be at different distances even when they are level?

▶ **What's wrong?**
Flashlights aren't shining straight at you? Raise one end with some modeling clay to level them out.

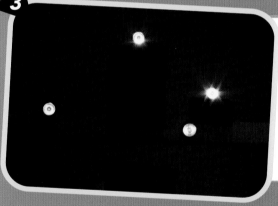

3 Move the boxes and flashlights to different distances from the front of the table but keep the constellation shape. Observe again.

▶ **Extra experiment**
Scatter some glitter stars on black poster board. Make them into a shape then photograph them. Look at the web site on page 30 to see how real constellations look in the sky.

▶ **Record**
Make a series of glittery constellations and photograph them. Show them to your friends. How many can they identify?

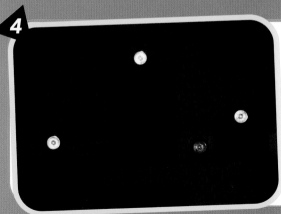

4 Replace the batteries in some of the flashlights with older ones, so that some shine more dimly than others. Repeat steps 2–3.

▶ **Think about it**
Would the constellations look the same to an alien on another planet orbiting another star?

Dwarfs and Giants

Most stars look like white dots to us, but when viewed through a powerful telescope (left) they actually vary in size and color. The smallest stars are red dwarfs. Next come orange stars, then yellow, then yellow-white, then blue-white stars. The largest stars are often called blue giants.

Red dwarfs sizzle at 5,432°F (3,000°C)! Blue giants are more than 10 times hotter still. During their lifetime, yellow stars swell to become red giants as they cool.

Get Going

The light from stars gets weaker as it travels toward Earth. When it reaches Earth's atmosphere, it has to fight through moving air masses. This makes the starlight twinkle when we see it from the ground. You can copy the effect using bubble wrap!

▲ This is the birth of a star. Every star has a lifetime. It shines for thousands of millions of years until its gas burns out. Then the star darkens and "dies."

1

Draw around the bulb end of each flashlight onto the poster board. Cut out the shapes. In the middle of each, cut a hole. The largest hole should be 1 in. (2.5 cm) across and the smallest about ½ in. (1 cm).

2

Stick blue cellophane across the largest hole, leave the next hole clear, then stick yellow over the next largest hole, orange next, then red over the smallest hole.

Science Box

Table, black poster board, 4 boxes of different heights, 5 flashlights, pencil, scissors, ruler, cellophane colored blue, yellow, red, and orange (or color in clear cellophane with marker pens), adhesive tape, piece of bubble wrap about 7 x 7 in. (18 x 18 cm).

3

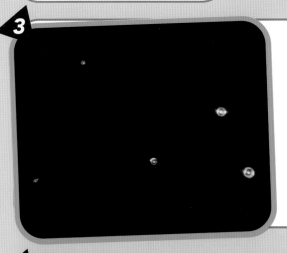

Stick the disks on the front of the flashlights. On the table, place one flashlight on each box—and one on the table top—in a constellation pattern. Darken the room and observe from the other end.

4

Hold out the bubble wrap at arm's length in front of you and move it up and down as you look at the "stars."

▶ **Observe**
Which color of star is easiest to see? Which is the most difficult?

▶ **Predict**
How might real stars look through the moving bubble wrap? Test your prediction.

▶ **Record**
Take a photograph of your colorful constellation. Can you film the effect of looking at it through the bubble wrap?

▶ **Think about it**
When a yellow star like the Sun uses up all its gas it cools down. What color does it go?

Birth of the Planets

The Sun in our sky is about 5 billion years old. It began, like other stars, as a spinning ball of gas and dust. Around the Sun, particles of dust crashed together and started to form lumps—and then huge chunks of rock. This is how all the planets in the solar system were formed.

Mars

Earth

Mercury

Venus

The four planets nearest to the Sun are rocky planets. Farther out, four rocky chunks were coated in huge balls of gas. These became the gas planets, or gas giants. A small lump of rock beyond them was coated in ice and formed what used to be called the ninth planet, Pluto.

Get Going

Use binoculars to look for planets in the night sky. You can tell a planet from a star because it shines with a steady light and doesn't twinkle. Now make a solar system mobile to hang in your room.

Swinging Solar System

▼ Some of the gases around the rocky cores of the gas giants (all four shown below) were pulled down by gravity toward their centers and crushed so hard they turned into liquids.

Neptune

Uranus

Saturn

Pluto is not shown in this illustration. Most scientists believe it is too small to be classified as a planet.

Jupiter

Science Box

A piece of poster board over 5½ in. (14 cm) square, ruler, compass, pencil, scissors, 10 pieces of thread 4 in. (10 cm) long, 4 pieces of thread about 12 in. (30 cm) long, adhesive tape, white poster board, paints or colored pencils, clear plastic cup, dish-washing liquid, spoon, marble, 2 freezer bags, modeling clay, 4 tablespoons of sand, 12 small nails, water.

1

Use the ruler and compass to mark out circles with the following diameters, one inside the other, on the poster board: 5½, 5, 4½, 4, 3½, 3, 2½, 2, 1½, 1 in. (13, 12.5, 11.5, 10.5, 9.5, 8.5, 6.5, 5.5, 4.5, 3.5 cm).

2

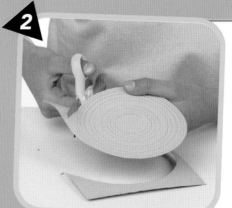

Cut around the 5-in. (13-cm) circle.
Continues on the next page.

3

Mark the positions of the planets on the inner circles, as shown on pages 12–13. The center of the disk, where the point of the compass went, is the position of the Sun.

4

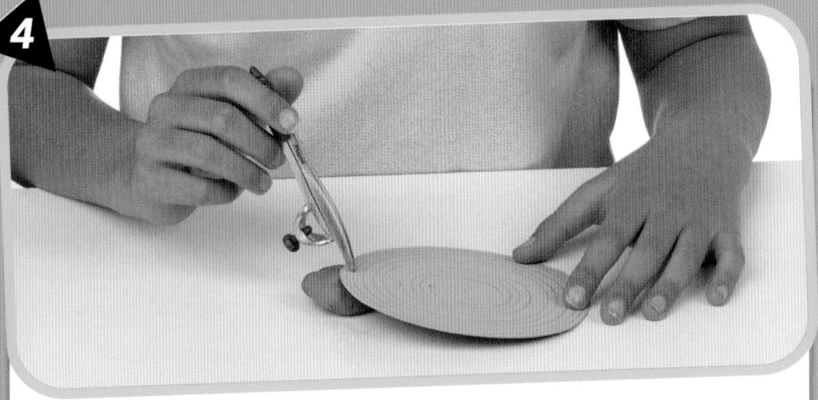

Carefully make holes for the planets (include Pluto if you want) and Sun using the point of the compass (place modeling clay underneath). Make the holes larger by pushing the point of the pencil through.

5

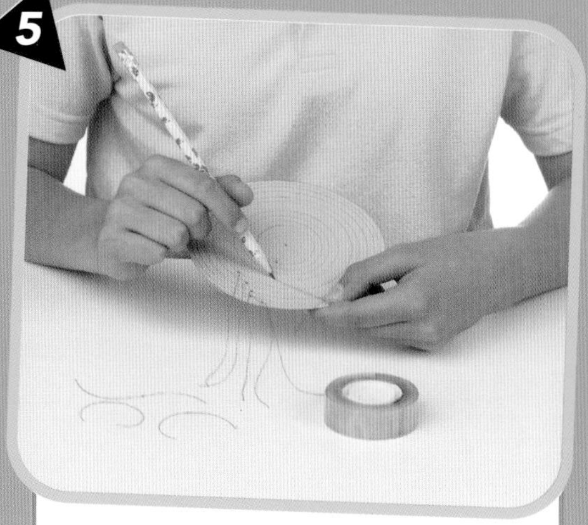

Poke a thread through each hole so that about ½ in. (1 cm) goes through. Stick this down with tape.

6

Make drawings of the Sun and planets to a very rough scale on the white card. Look at pictures of the planets to help you color them in on both sides. Note that Jupiter's red spot is on one side only.

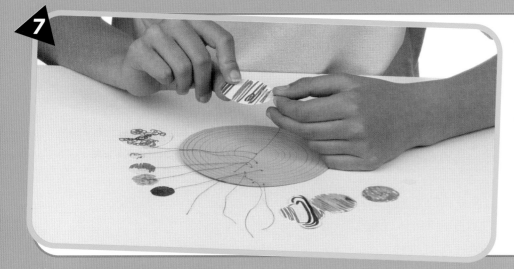

7

Attach the Sun and planets to the threads using adhesive tape. Make sure you keep all the planets at the same height—in line with the middle of the Sun.

8

Tape one end of each long thread at four points on the other side of the card and hold up your solar system mobile.

▶ **Observe**
Note the colors, sizes, and positions of each planet and see how many things you can say about the differences between any two planets.

▶ **Predict**
What would happen to a space probe landing on a gas planet? To test your prediction, froth up some water and dish-washing liquid in a cup, then drop in a marble.

▶ **Extra experiment**
Put two tablespoons of sand in a freezer bag. Mix in some nails and add water until the sand is very damp. Repeat with another bag, but leave out the nails. Leave the bags in a warm place such as an airing cupboard for a week, then empty each bag and compare.

▶ **Think about it**
Planets don't give off light themselves, so how do they shine?

Circling the Sun

When you jump up, you fall back down. This is the work of gravity, a force that pulls you toward Earth. Gravity acts on every object in the universe. Its strength depends on the object's size. The Sun is so big that its gravity pulls on all the planets and stops them from spinning away into space.

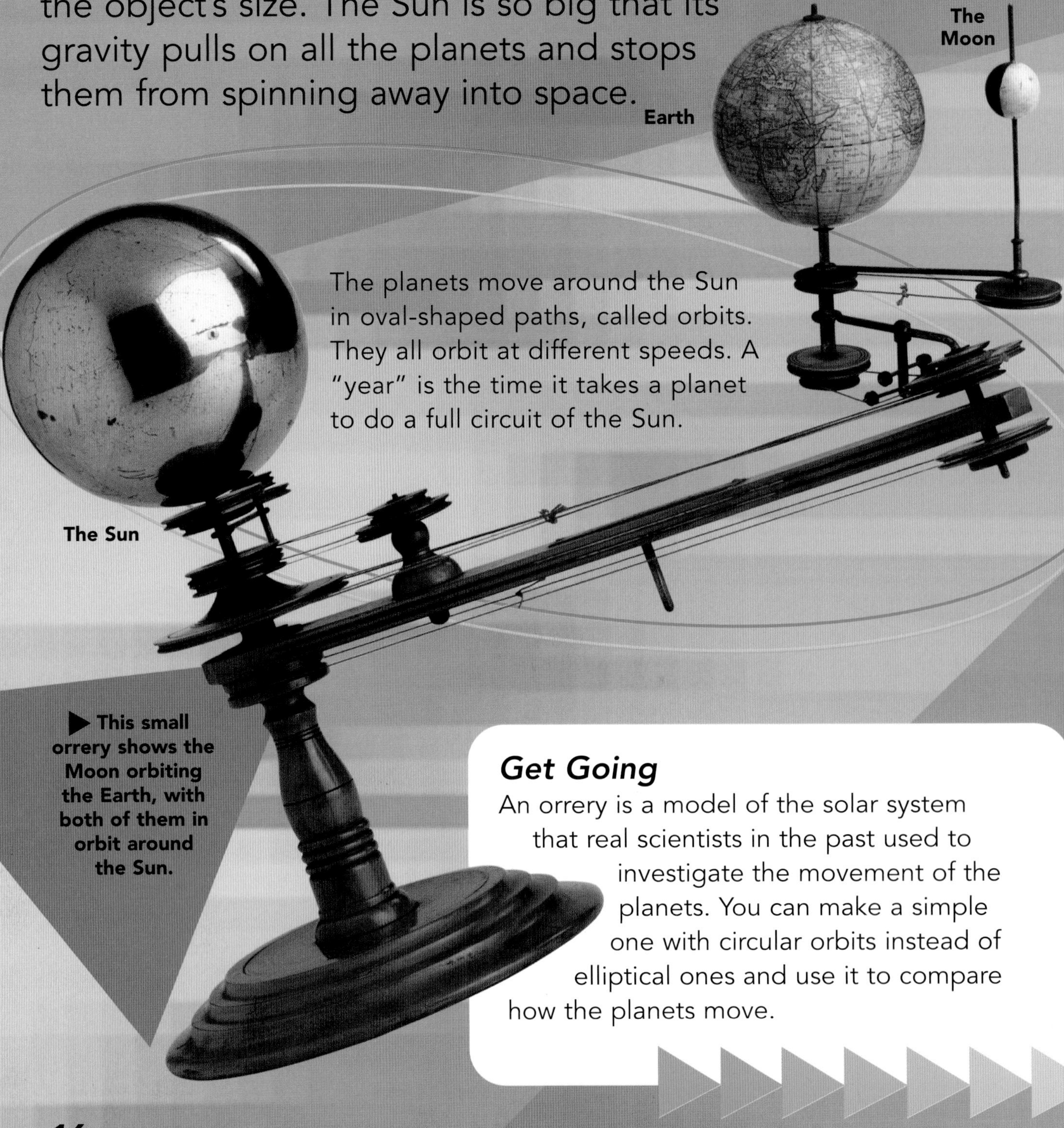

The Moon

Earth

The planets move around the Sun in oval-shaped paths, called orbits. They all orbit at different speeds. A "year" is the time it takes a planet to do a full circuit of the Sun.

The Sun

▶ This small orrery shows the Moon orbiting the Earth, with both of them in orbit around the Sun.

Get Going

An orrery is a model of the solar system that real scientists in the past used to investigate the movement of the planets. You can make a simple one with circular orbits instead of elliptical ones and use it to compare how the planets move.

1 Use the ruler and compasses to make ten poster board circles with diameters of 9½, 8½, 8, 7, 6½, 5½, 4½, 4, 3, and 2 in. (24, 22, 20, 18, 16, 14, 12, 10, 8, and 5 cm).

Science Box

Large pieces of poster board, ruler, pair of compasses, pencil, scissors, round-head solid brass paper fasteners, adhesive tape, stopwatch or other timer, piece of string, table tennis ball.

2

3  Cut nine poster board strips, ¼ in. wide by 2 in. long (1 cm wide by 4 cm long). Bend them in the middle. Attach one to the edge of each circle with adhesive tape.

Cut out the circles and make a small hole in the center of each. Pile up the circles starting with the largest at the bottom. Link them with the round-head fastener through the middle.

4  Draw each of the planets on a piece of card, using your solar system mobile as a guide. Cut them out and attach them to the card strips in order, with Mercury on the smallest ring and Pluto on the largest.

▶ **Observe**
Think of the round-head fastener as the Sun. Gently move each planet around it in a counterclockwise direction.

▶ **Record**
Time how long it takes you to move Mercury one full circle. Repeat with each planet in turn. Record your results in a table and compare.

▶ **What's wrong?**
Poster board disks are sticking? Turn them around a few times before you make your planet movements.

▶ **Think about it**
Do the real planets stay in line as they go around the Sun?

▶ **Extra experiment**
Can you spin a ball like the Sun spins a planet? Attach a piece of string to a table tennis ball, hold it at arm's length, and try to make the ball spin around your hand. What would happen if you let go of the string?

Moon Motion

Many scientists believe that another planet crashed into Earth as the solar system was forming. Chunks of rock were flung out from Earth and spun in a ring around it. Gradually, the chunks crashed together and made a rock about one-quarter the size of Earth. This became the Moon.

The Moon orbits Earth at a slight angle to Earth's orbit around the Sun. This means that for most of the time they are not in line. Sometimes the Moon is slightly above the level of the Sun and Earth, and sometimes it is below it.

▲ On rare occasions, the Sun, Moon, and Earth line up and an eclipse occurs. A solar eclipse (above) is when the Moon comes between Earth and the Sun. In a lunar eclipse, Earth comes between the Sun and the Moon. **NEVER LOOK DIRECTLY AT THE SUN.**

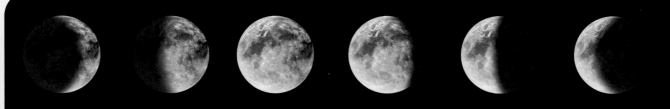

Get Going

As the Moon moves around the Earth, we see different amounts of its surface lit by the Sun. The lit-up areas, which change nightly, are called phases of the Moon. Make a model to see them in action.

1 Draw a circle, 5½ in. (14 cm) in diameter, on poster board and cut it out. Cut out a square, 6 x 6 in. (16 x 16 cm), from the other piece of board. Place the circle over the square and push a fastener through the middle.

Science box

2 large sheets of poster board, compass, pencil, ruler, scissors, round-head solid brass paper fastener, metallic pen or white pencil, ball of modeling clay 1 in. (2–3 cm) in diameter, flashlight, spare lump of modeling clay.

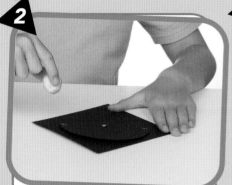

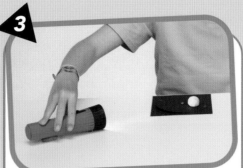

2 Mark opposite sides of the circular card with an M (for Moon) and E (for Earth). Press the ball of modeling clay onto the place marked M.

3 Place the model near the edge of a table and shine the flashlight from about 6 in. (16 cm) away, making an angle of about 45 degrees with the table edge. Use the spare modeling clay to make the light shine horizontally.

► Observe

How much of the ball can you see lit up in the first part of step 4? How does this change as your viewpoint at E moves closer to the flashlight?

► Record

Draw four pictures of the lit surface of the ball as you move it around a quarter circle each time. Label which you think is a New Moon and which is a Full Moon.

► Predict

As a New Moon gradually changes to a Full Moon, it is said to be waxing. When the reverse happens, it is waning. Look at the Moon and make a drawing of it every night for a week. Predict how the Moon will look next and make a drawing. Is it waxing or waning? Check it the following night.

► Think about it

What would you see if you were on Earth, on the side facing the Moon, as shown in the photo for step 4?

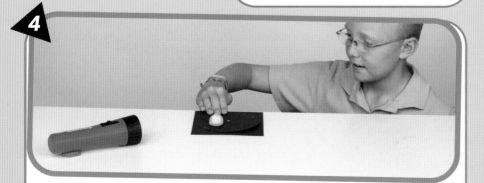

4 Turn the circular card so the ball is nearest to the flashlight, crouch down, and look at it from the point marked E. Move the card counterclockwise and change your position so you keep looking at the ball from E.

Space Rubble

Zooming around the solar system are bits of stuff that never became planets or moons. Asteroids are chunks of rock up to 400 miles (600 km) wide. Comets are balls of ice and dust that grow gassy "tails" when they get close to the Sun and start to melt.

Most asteroids lie in a "belt" around the Sun, between the orbits of Mars and Jupiter. Comets have oval orbits that swing in from the edge of the solar system, around the Sun, and away again.

▲ Occasionally an asteroid, like the one above, or a comet goes off track and crashes into a planet or moon. The crater below is in Arizona, and was made by a meteorite strike 20,000–50,000 years ago.

Get Going

Asteroids and comets that reach Earth's surface are known as meteorites. Make your own meteorites and examine the craters they make.

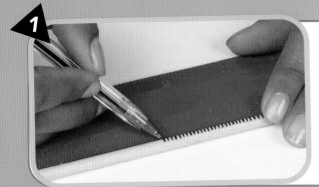

Crashing Craters

1

Mark out ⅛ in. (2 mm) lines on the piece of dowel. You will use this to measure the crater depth.

Science Box

Piece of dowel about 3 in. (8 cm) long, ruler, pen, flour, lumps of modeling clay or pebbles of various sizes, large box or high-sided tray, newspaper, safety glasses.

2

Spread out some newspaper and place the box on top. Pour in the flour and make sure it is at least 2 in. (5 cm) deep. Flatten the surface by scraping it with the ruler.

3

Put on the safety glasses. Hold a modeling clay "meteorite" 20 in. (50 cm) above the box, and then let it drop.

4

Measure the width of the crater, then carefully lift out the meteorite. Put one end of the dowel into the crater to measure its depth.

▶ **Observe**
Drop each of your meteorites into the flour one at a time, always from the same height. Smooth the flour surface before each drop. Compare the crater measurements.

▶ **Predict**
What would happen to the crater size if you dropped the same meteorite from higher up or lower down? Test your prediction.

▶ **Record**
Make a table of your crater measurements. Take photographs of the craters and compare them.

▶ **Think about it**
Do faster-moving meteorites make deeper craters than slower-moving ones? How does the size of a meteorite affect the size of the crater it makes?

Seasons of the Sun

We can't feel it, but Earth is spinning all the time. It spins around an imaginary line, or axis, that runs between the North and South Poles. The side of Earth facing the Sun has daylight, while on the other side it is night. The axis is slightly tilted and points in the same direction all the time the Earth orbits the Sun.

When a Pole points toward the Sun, the Sun rises high in the sky in that half of the world and the days are longer. This is summer. When a Pole points away from the Sun, the Sun stays lower in the sky and the days are shorter. This is winter.

▼ The Sun always sets in the west. But it doesn't move or go out—the Sun just slowly disappears from sight as the Earth rotates.

Get Going

As the Earth rotates during the daytime, the Sun appears to move across the sky. You can trace the path of the Sun by watching where it casts shadows. Never look directly at the Sun—it can seriously damage your eyes.

1

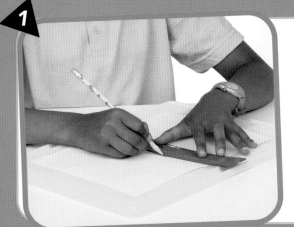

Stick the white paper to the board with adhesive tape. Mark halfway down one long side and draw a line straight across the paper to the other side.

Science Box

Wooden or plastic board, white paper, adhesive tape, ruler, 2 pencils, compass, piece of modeling clay, clock.

2

Stand a pencil in the modeling clay at one end of the line across the paper.

3

Find an open space where there are no shadows from buildings or trees. Find north on the compass and set the board with the pencil side to the south (or north if you are in the southern hemisphere).

4

At 8 A.M. on a sunny day, mark the length of the pencil's shadow on the paper. Repeat every hour until 4 P.M.

▶ **Observe**
How did the shadow length change in the morning? How did it change in the afternoon?

▶ **Record**
Make a table showing the time and the shadow length.

▶ **Predict**
How do you think the results would compare in a month's time? Set up a new shadow clock to test your prediction.

▶ **What's wrong?**
Cloud developing? Take measurements whenever you can as the clouds pass by.

▶ **Think about it**
When the Sun is low in the sky, shadows are long. They get shorter as the Sun rises to its highest point. How could you draw the path of the Sun across the sky from the shadow lengths on your shadow clock?

Speedy Spacecraft

You need to be quick to get into space. Spacecraft must travel at 25,000 mph (40,000 km/h) to escape the strong pull of Earth's gravity. Powerful rocket engines launch a spacecraft from the ground, burning huge amounts of fuel, and letting off jets of hot gas. The gas blazes downward and, as it does so, a strong upward force pushes back.

Once a spacecraft reaches space, the fuel tanks and rocket engines are released and fall back to Earth. Smaller tanks and engines keep the spacecraft going while it is in space.

▲ The NASA space shuttle is one of the most successful spacecraft with more than 120 launches into space.

◀ Most spacecraft carry astronauts. They will experience "weightlessness" because there is no gravity in space. Astronauts use scientific instruments to measure conditions in space.

Get Going
A balloon releases a jet of gas when it deflates, and a force pushes it forward all over the place. You can make a balloon rocket travel in a straight line by using a straw and a string.

1

Cut the straw into three equal parts and put two of them onto the thread.

Science Box

Plastic straw, ruler, scissors, 10 ft. (3 m) piece of thread, long balloon, balloon pump, binder clip, adhesive tape, cupboard handle or top of a door, empty matchbox.

2

3

Blow up the balloon and hold the end shut with a binder clip. Bring the balloon to the pieces of straw and stick one piece to the back and the other to the front.

Tie the end of the thread at the front of the balloon to a high point. Move the balloon to the lower end of the thread, make a prediction, then release the binder clip.

▶ **Predict**
What will happen when you release the balloon at the end of step 3? Test your prediction.

▶ **Observe**
What happens to the balloon and payload when the balloon deflates in step 4?

▶ **Record**
Use a camcorder to film the rocket action in both activities.

▶ **What's wrong?**
Balloon and payload stick? Check that the straws can move smoothly along the thread.

▶ **Think about it**
Rockets don't push on the air to make them move as some people used to think. If this was true, what would happen to rockets when they fired in space?

4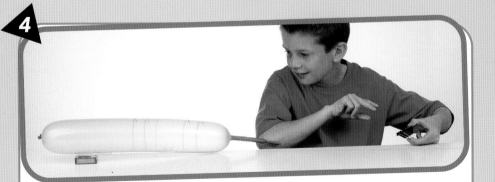

Insert the third piece of straw in front of the balloon and attach the matchbox (the payload section) to it. Fasten the end of the thread to a lower object so the thread can be held horizontally. Inflate the balloon and release it.

Looking for Life

As far as we know, there is no life anywhere but on Earth. But space scientists are still looking for life elsewhere. They know that living things on Earth need water, warmth, and food, so they test other planets and moons for signs like these too. In 1976, the first major test for life was made by two spacecraft that landed on Mars.

▲ After the Big Bang, shown here at a space exhibition, the first forms of life on Earth were microbes. Some scientists think they formed from chemicals in the first seas, while others think they may have started out as space dust.

▲ This illustration shows rover "Opportunity" on Mars in 2004. Rovers can investigate planet conditions, such as the types of rock and the kinds of weather. The data that Opportunity provides may help scientists to discover life on Mars.

Get Going

Scientists hoped that the soil of Mars would froth with gas as any life forms fed. Yeast is really a fungus, but can you get it to behave like possible extraterrestrial life?

Alien Yeast

1

Put five teaspoons of sand in the cup and add one teaspoon of dried yeast. Stir it up.

Science Box

Clear plastic cup, food dye, teaspoon, dry sand, packet of dried yeast, sugar, warm water, ruler, bowl.

2

Add half a teaspoon of sugar to the cup.

3

Add a few drops of food dye to the warm water and pour it in to a depth of 1¼ in. (3 cm). Stir everything together.

4

Place the cup in a bowl of warm water for half an hour.

▶ **Observe**
Look at the mixture every few minutes and describe what you see.

▶ **Record**
Take a photograph every five minutes of the cup and its contents.

▶ **Fair test**
How could you be sure that sand and sugar alone don't produce the same result? Figure out a test and try it.

▶ **What's wrong?**
No change in the contents of the cup? Add more sugar and make the water a little warmer (but not hot). Cup falls over in the bowl of water? Pour some water out of the bowl.

▶ **Think about it**
Scientists looking for large life forms on other planets look for a gas that animals on Earth need, too. Take a breath and think what this gas is.

Looking for Life **27**

Results and Answers

Page 7 Blow Up Universe

The galaxies move farther apart as the universe expands. Many scientists believe that the universe will continue to expand forever. In the past, however, it was thought that it would contract again in a process called The Big Crunch (as the balloon deflates). Some scientists believed that all the stuff in the universe would disappear completely into a huge black hole. Of course, these are just theories.

Page 9 Cool Constellations

The bulbs will seem to be at the same distance if they are all the same brightness. A bright star will appear to be nearer even if it is farther away. A constellation will look different from a different viewpoint on another planet around another star.

Page 11 Twinkling Stars

Yellow stars are the easiest to see, and red stars may be the most difficult to see. The flashlight flickers as you move the bubble wrap, demonstrating why stars appear to twinkle when viewed through Earth's atmosphere. When a yellow star uses up its gas and cools down it becomes a red giant.

Page 15 Swinging Solar System

The planets are in line with Mercury nearest the Sun, then Venus, Earth, Mars, Jupiter, Saturn, Uranus, Neptune, and Pluto. The marble space probe goes straight through the gas (froth) and into the liquid. The center of the gas giants is liquid—there is no solid surface to land on. As a space probe sinks into a gas giant, the pressure increases so much that it is crushed. The nails rust and give the sand a brown-red color in the same way that Martian sand is red because of the rusting of iron in it when the planet had water on its surface. Light from the Sun makes the planets appear to shine.

Page 17 Ready, Steady...Orrery!

It may take about three to five seconds to turn Mercury around the Sun. As you move outward, it takes longer for each planet to make an orbit. The real planets do not move in line, or in circular orbits. The pull between your hand and the spinning ball is similar in some ways to the pull of gravity. When you let go, the ball flies off. If gravity was suddenly to cease to exist (which it won't) all the parts of the solar system would drift away into space.

Page 19 Lunar Loops

The flashlight's light on the ball begins as a crescent, or New Moon, then moves to Half Moon, Full Moon, Half Moon, and then a crescent at the other side of the ball. The Earth (you) and Moon appear to move as if the same part of Earth is always facing the Moon—even though this does not actually happen. Earth spins around once every 24 hours and the Moon takes nearly 30 days to orbit Earth. The Moon makes 12 Earth orbits in the time it takes Earth to orbit the Sun once. In Think about it, if you were on Earth facing the Moon with the Sun behind it, you would see a solar eclipse.

Page 21 Crashing Craters

A meteorite makes a wider, deeper crater when dropped from a higher height than the same meteorite does from a lower height. Gravity makes objects speed up as they fall. If you drop meteorites from a low height above the flour, they will not have speeded up much when they hit its surface, and will make a small, shallow crater. If they fall from a higher height, they will speed up more before they hit the flour and make a wider, deeper crater. In Think about it, yes, faster moving meteorites do make deeper craters. Usually, the bigger a meteorite is, the larger the crater will be—but this also depends on the material the meteorite is made of. Metal meteorites, for example, will make the biggest craters of all.

Page 23 Shadow Clock

The shadow shortened during the morning to a minimum at noon. The shadow lengthened during the afternoon. If the first shadow clock is set up after midwinter or in the spring, in the following month, the noon shadow will be shorter as the Sun rises higher in the sky. If the first shadow clock is set up after midsummer or in the fall, in the following month, the noon shadow will be longer since the Sun does not rise as high in the sky. You can plot the Sun's course in the following way: on a second sheet of paper, draw out the lengths of the shadows in height order, and in parallel lines. Turn the paper so the lines hang down and draw a line from the tip of each one to make an arc across the paper.

Page 25 Balloon Blastoff!

The rocket should shoot up the thread and perhaps reach the end of it. If the balloon and payload don't reach the end of the thread before the balloon deflates, then the inflated balloon should stop before the payload section and the payload section should separate and move ahead of the balloon. The rockets would not move because there is no air in space against which the gases could push. The forces in a rocket engine follow Newton's third law of motion, which says that to every action (the pushing force of the gases as they escape from the rocket) there is an equal and opposite reaction (the force which pushes the rocket forward).

Page 27 Alien Yeast

As the yeast feeds on the sugar, it uses the energy in the sugar, respires, and produces carbon dioxide gas. This forms bubbles in the water and may form a froth on the water surface. In a fair test, just five teaspoons of dried sand would be tested with the warm water and sugar. If you test just sand and sugar, there should not be any production of bubbles or froth. The gas animals need to breathe is oxygen.

Further Information

Look at these web sites for more information on our solar system and beyond:

▶ *http://hubblesite.org/gallery/album/galaxy_collection*
Log onto this web site to see some amazing pictures of different kinds of galaxies.

▶ *http://www.astroviewer.com*
Find out about the constellations on view in the night sky in various parts of the world by logging onto this web site.

▶ *http://www.nasa.gov*
Home page of NASA, the North American Space Agency.

▶ *http://www.kidsastronomy.com/solar_system.htm*
Watch the planets, asteroids, and comets move around the Sun at this web site.

▶ *http://www.extrasolar.net*
This web page describes extrasolar planets (planets that orbit other stars).

▶ *http://science.nationalgeographic.com/science/space/solar-system/asteroids-comets-article.html*
Find out about asteroids and comets at this interactive web site.

▶ *http://pbskids.org/zoom/activities/sci/lemonjuicerockets.html*
Ask an adult to read through this web page with you and help you make and fire the rocket. Remember you need to wear safety glasses.

▶ *http://marsprogram.jpl.nasa.gov/MPF/mpf/education/cutouts.html*
Make a model of the Mars "Pathfinder" spacecraft to discover how complicated space probes are.

▶ *http://coolcosmos.ipac.caltech.edu//cosmic_kids/AskKids/index.shtml*
The science of studying the universe is called astronomy. Find out more about astronomy on this web site.

▶ *http://www.nineplanets.org*
Find out about the details of the planets in the solar system at this web site.

Every effort has been made by the Publishers to ensure that these web sites contain no inappropriate or offensive material. However, because of the nature of the Internet, it is impossible to guarantee that the contents of these sites will not be altered. We strongly advise that Internet access is supervised by a responsible adult.

Glossary

Alien
A living thing that is not from Earth but may live on another planet or moon.

Astronaut
A person who is specially trained to live and work in space.

Big Bang
The explosion believed to have occurred when the universe formed.

Constellation
A shape or pattern in the sky made by a group of stars in the Milky Way galaxy.

Diameter
The line across a circle, from one side to the other, through the center.

Fuel
A substance that is burned to provide power for movement or heat.

Galaxy
A huge group of millions of stars in space.

Gas giant
A planet that has a rocky center but is mainly composed of gas. In the solar system, Jupiter, Saturn, Uranus, and Neptune are gas giants.

Gravity
A force of attraction that occurs between any two objects in the universe. It only causes movement when one of the objects is very much larger than the other.

Orbit
The path taken by a planet around a star or a moon around a planet.

Planet
A large object that moves in an orbit around a star.

Radio telescope
A telescope that detects radio waves instead of light waves from space and converts them into images.

Rotate
To turn around an axis the same way a wheel turns around an axle.

Shadow
A dark area behind an object where rays of light from a light source, such as the Sun or a flashlight, cannot reach.

Solar system
The Sun, and all the objects that are in the pull of its gravity, such as planets with their moons, the asteroids, and comets.

Space station
A large structure orbiting Earth in which astronauts live and work.

Star
A huge ball of gas made from hydrogen and helium.

Universe
All of space and everything that is in it, including galaxies of stars and the planets, moons, and other objects that go around them.

Index

To my granddaughter Pippa May

This edition first published in 2011 by Sea-to-Sea Publications
Distributed by Black Rabbit Books
P.O. Box 3263, Mankato, Minnesota 56002

Text copyright © Peter Riley 2008, 2011
Design and concept © Sea-to-Sea Publications 2011
Printed in China, Dongguan
All rights reserved.

Library of Congress Cataloging-in-Publication Data
Riley, Peter D.
  Space / Peter Riley.
    p. cm. -- (The real scientist investigates)
  Includes index.
  ISBN 978-1-59771-284-2 (lib. bdg.)
 1. Astronomy--Juvenile literature. 2. Astronomy--Experiments--Juvenile literature. 3. Astrophysics--Experiments--Juvenile literature. 4. Science--Methodology--Juvenile literature. I.Title.
  QB46.R574 2011
  520.78--dc22
                                    2010005375

9 8 7 6 5 4 3 2

Published by arrangement with the Watts Publishing Group Ltd., London.

Editor: Susie Brooks
Series Editor: Adrian Cole
Art Director: Jonathan Hair
Design: Matthew Lilly
Picture Research: Diana Morris
Photography: Andy Crawford (unless otherwise credited)

Acknowledgments:
The Band/Shutterstock: 18b. Adrian Bradshaw/epa/Corbis: 26t. Andrea Danti/Shutterstock: cover tc, cr. DK Ltd/Corbis: 3t, 16. Luke Dodd/SPL: 8t. Jeanne Hatch/Shutterstock cover br. Holland Ford (JHU)/ACS Science Team/ESA/NASA: 2cl, 10b. Laurence Gough/Shutterstock: 2tl, 5t. Jodrell Bank, University of Manchester: 8b. JPL/NASA: 1, 2bl, 3bc, 12-13, 26b. Alexander Kolomietz/Shutterstock: cover tr. NASA: 2tr, 3cl, 4cl, 6, 20t. NASA/SPL: 24bl. Alex Neauville/Shutterstock: 20b. Svetlana Privezentseva/Shutterstock: cover bcr. Michael Ransburg/Shutterstock: cover bl. Detlar van Ravenswaay /SPL: 24tr. Roger Ressmeyer/Corbis: 10t, 18t. Spectral-Design/Shutterstock: cover tl. STS-116 Shuttle Crew/NASA: 4. Birute Vijeikiene/Shutterstock: 3cr, 22.

Every attempt has been made to clear copyright. Should there be any inadvertent omission please apply to the publisher for rectification.

March 2010
RD/6000006414/002